# UNTIED KNOTS

Sven Waldemar Swenson

Untied Knots

ISBN 978-1-64538-039-9
First Edition

Untied Knots
by Sven Waldemar Swenson



For information, please contact:

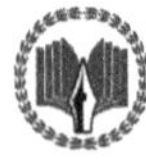

Orange Hat Publishing
www.orangehatpublishing.com
Waukesha, WI

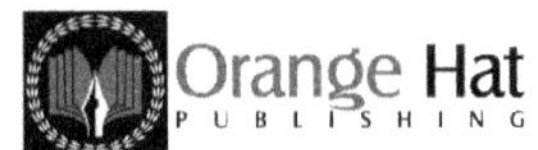

## *Dedication*

*This book is dedicated to Sven and the legacy he has provided for his family. Thank you for choosing me to ensure your moments in time are not forgotten.*

*-Arlys Swenson, Great-granddaughter*

# *WISCONSIN*

*Wisconsin, Land of Pines, where whip-poor-wills*
*And orioles and bluebirds sing*
*Their songs of joy o'er dales and hills,*
*Our hearts a thrill they bring.*

*You'll have to search the entire world before*
*You find a place of equal worth*
*To this - it's right here at your door -*
*This wonderland up north.*

*Here is the land of streams and lakes and pines,*
*Where trilliums grow and deer abound,*
*Where setting sun in glory shines*
*And song of birds resound.*

*Right here you'll find that certain creek or stream,*
*That very placid sky blue lake,*
*Where true will come your fondest dream*
*When record fish you take.*

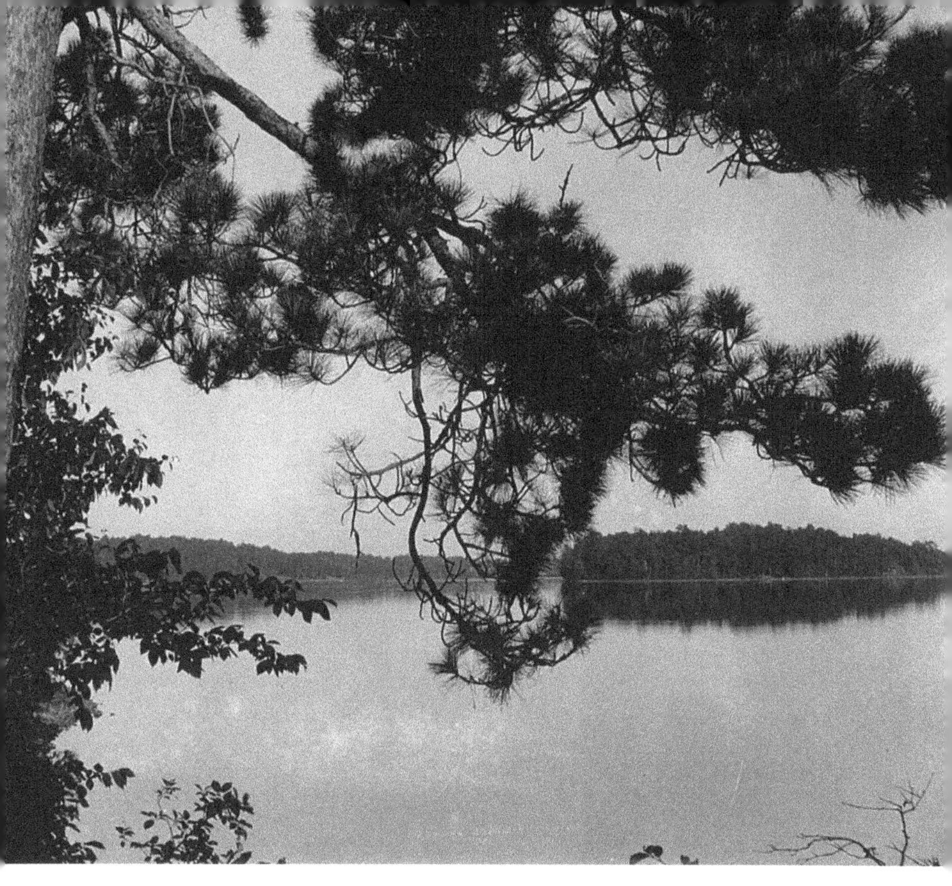

*Come out and roam the woods, where violets grow,*
*When startles grouse goes thundering by,*
*When rosy rays from sunsets glow*
*Still linger in the sky,*

*Come up and see me - bring a friend along,*
*You'll find at last your land of dreams,*
*Your heart will learn a sweeter song*
*Along the winding streams.*

# DAWN

*On waters calm spreads mystic light of dawn*
*In pastel shades of rose and silvery grey.*
*Across the bay a graceful spotted fawn*
*Bleats out a welcome to the newborn day.*

*A thousand birds tune in with jubilant song,*
*A pair of mallards in the rushes talk*
*And somewhere close the bittern sounds his gong*
*And soaring high above screams wily hawk.*

*The streamlined heron spreads his mighty wings*
*And floats majestically through the haze.*
*Out in the meadow yellow warbler sings*
*His sweetest song, the newborn day to praise.*

*All living things rejoice this morn,*
*In sheer delight and glee for new day born.*

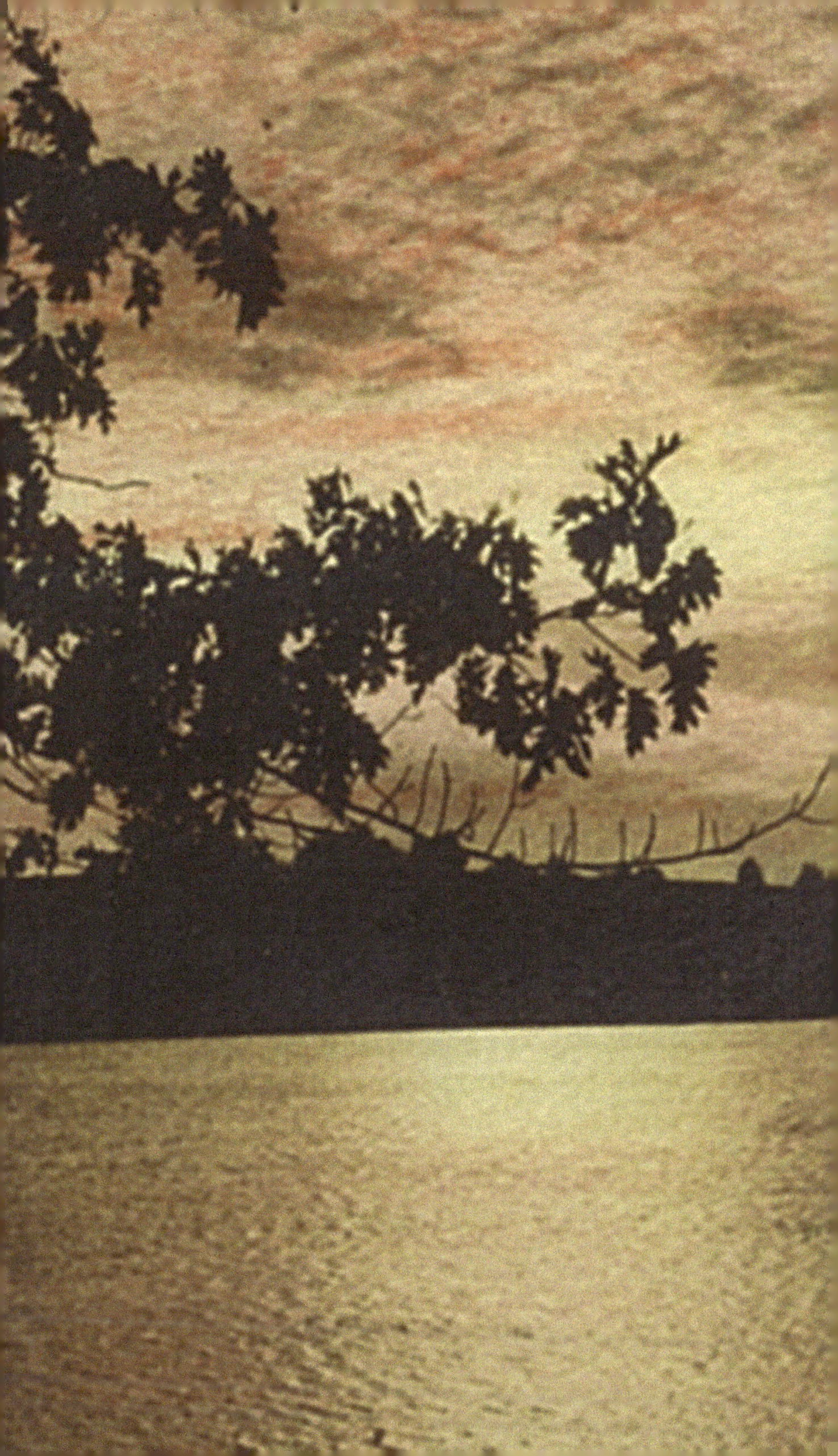

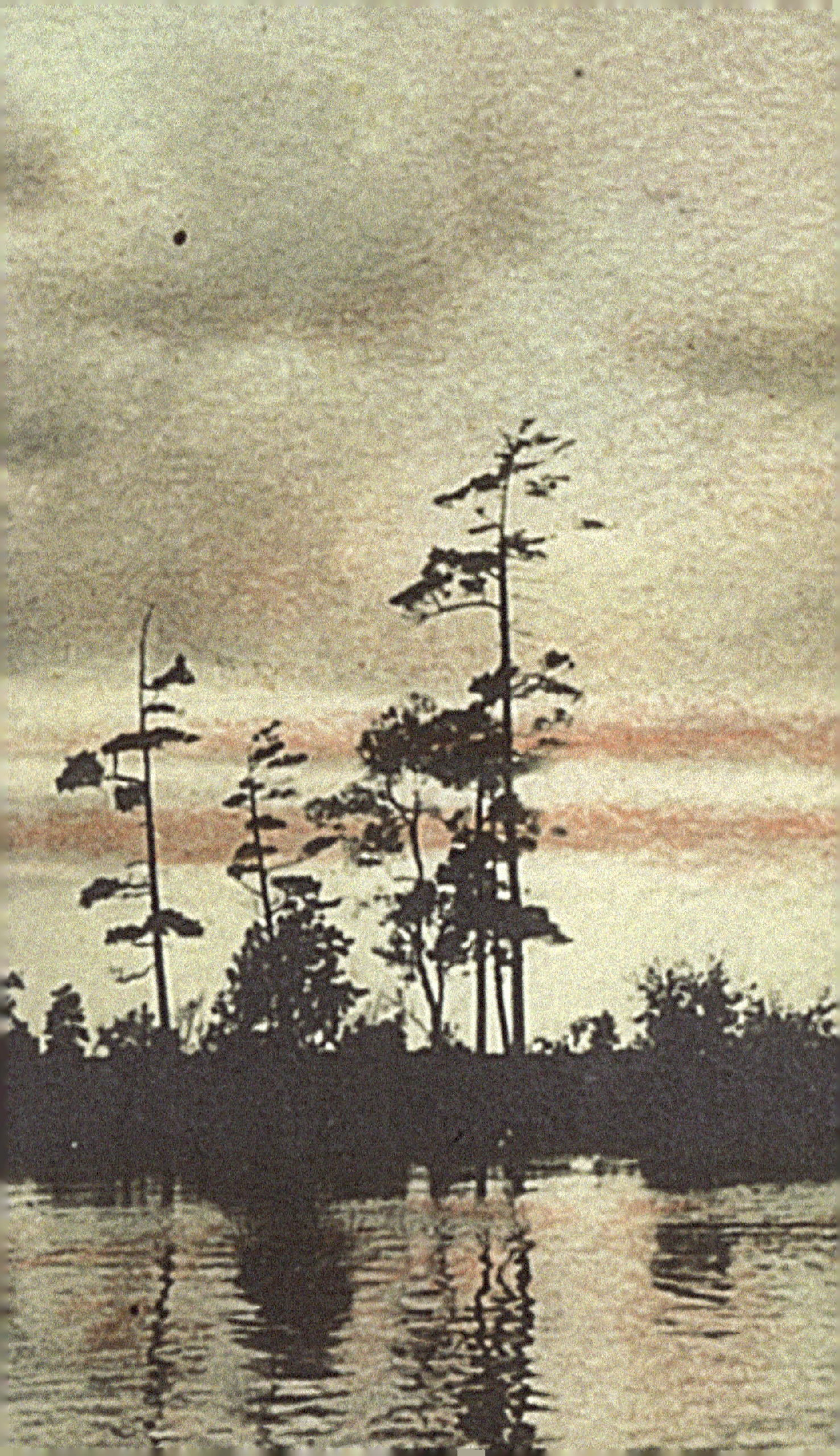

# *ANOTHER DAY IS BORN*

*Another day is born,*
*Who knows what it will bring,*
*Of gladness, joy,*
*Of pains,*
*Of sorrow, grief –*
*Of love,*
*Of hate,*
*Of dance and swing,*
*Of doubt and hope,*
*Of disbelief –*

# FLOWERS IN THE SPRING

*Wild-cherry blossoms on swaying limb,*
*Bending in graceful bow,*
*Reaching so softly o'er still pools rim,*
*Admiring beauty below.*

*Trilliums are nodding in glossy white,*
*(Just slightly touched with rose)*
*Open their petals and reach for light,*
*Tranquil and quiet repose.*

*Calta Palustris in yellow gold,*
*Background of deepest green,*
*Showy in contrast and daring, bold,*
*Their foliage of oily sheen.*

*Flowers in bloom, with enchantment, charm,*
*Tell us that spring is here.*
*Please do not gather them, don't do them harm,*
*They'll only wither and sear.*

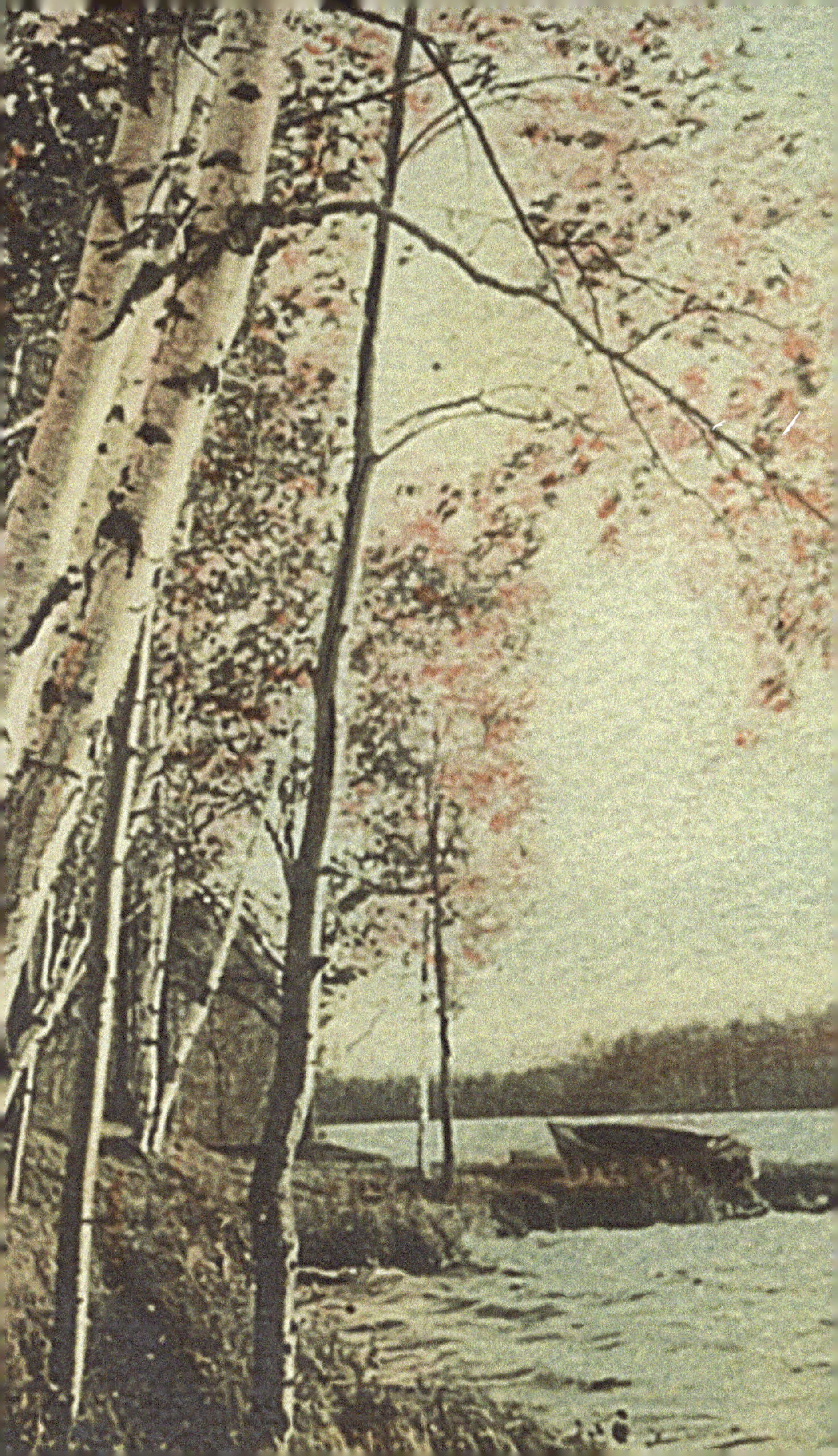

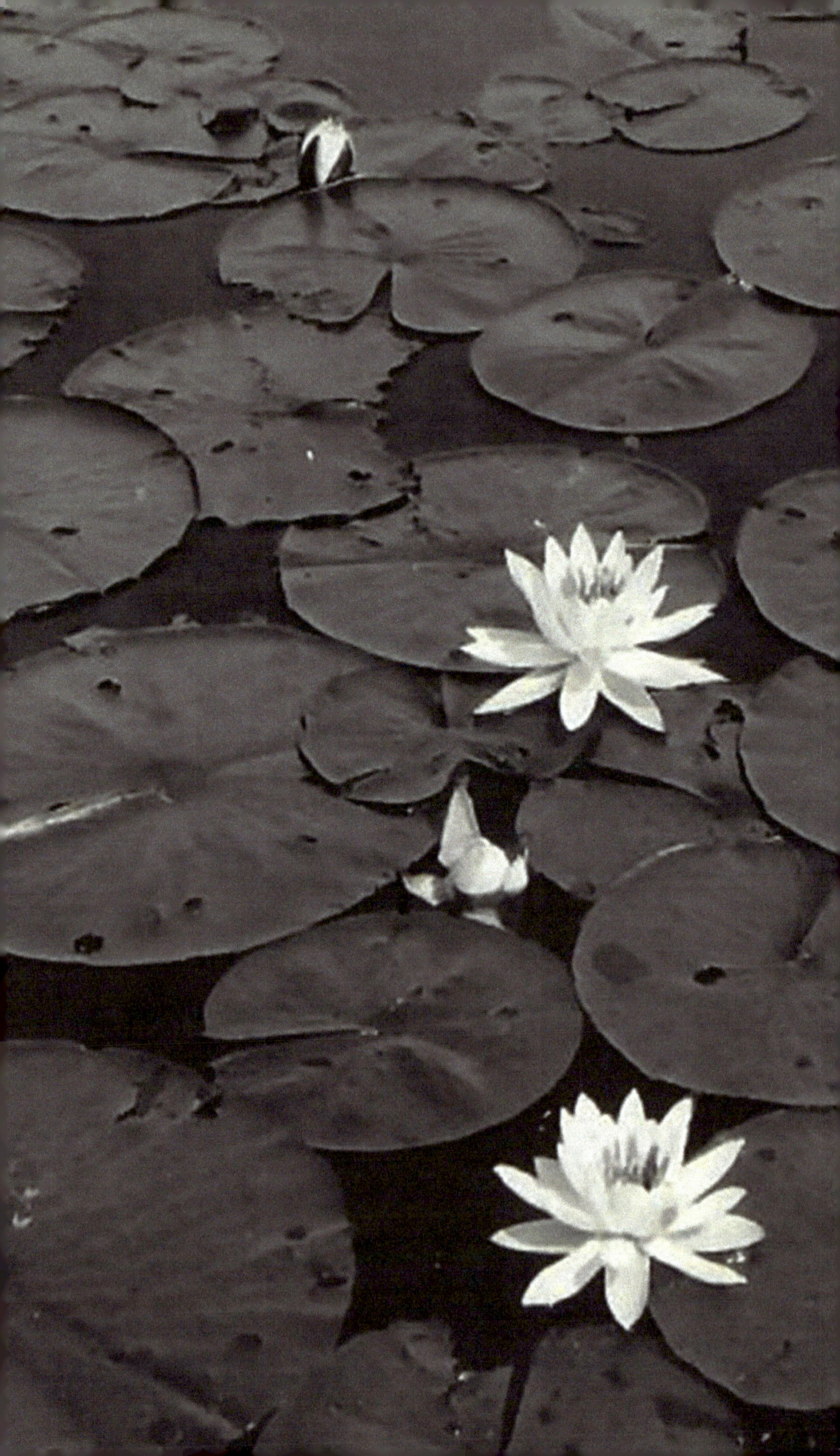

# *SONG OF THE LILIES*

*Oh! Beautiful lilies that rest on the pool,*
*A hymnal of pureness you sing.*
*A cupful of petals, white, sparkling and cool,*
*Corella like butterfly's wing.*

*"THE SPLENDOR OF GOD'S HANDYWORK"*

*Your song is mysterious, lingering and mild,*
*So placid and soft and so calm.*
*A tranquil message from out of the wild,*
*Like whispering, exulting psalm.*

*"THE SPLENDOR OF GOD'S HANDYWORK"*

# *AFTER THE RAIN*

*For many a week it was blistering hot,*
*A terrible, scorching, impetuous drought.*
*The grass and the flowers, the leaves on the trees,*
*Were withering fast in the hot drying breeze.*

*AND THEN CAME THE RAIN! – So refreshing and cool,*
*It's every drop was a life-saving pool.*
*It rained for an hour, then suddenly ceased*
*And now, all at once, the whole world seems released.*

*There's joy in the air and the birds take to wing,*
*Their breasts fairly bursting with joy and to sing*
*Their thanks for this wonderful cooling rain,*
*For health and for strength to our land again.*

*The dark clouds split open, from out in the west,*
*Came glorious sunshine, in brilliantly dressed,*
*The Old Sol himself seems so happy again*
*And thankful for wonderous, health-giving rain.*

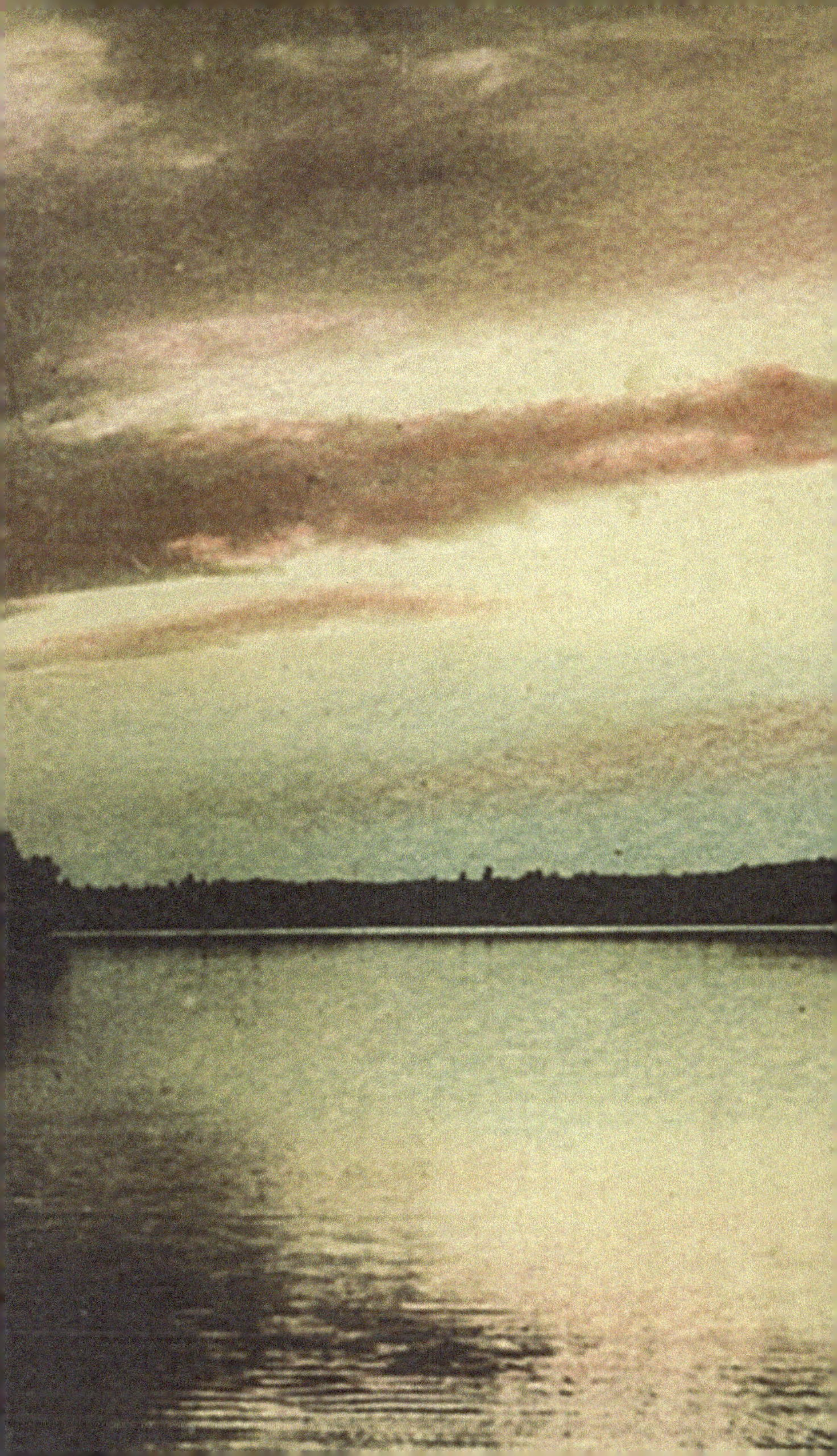

# *THE ANGLER*

*The stream at dawn. A mist of sheerest lace.*
*A breeze – And aspen leaves are shivering sweet.*
*The sound of fragrant dew-drops falling in the haze,*
*Like patter of a million elfin feet.*

*The breaking light, in pearl and palest blue,*
*In lavender and orange and tender rose.*
*A billion tiny diamonds form the dew,*
*A flock of songbirds wake from sweet repose.*

*Quite spellbound by the beauty of it all*
*The Angler stands. He drops his rod and reel,*
*Forgets about his flies and lures et al,*
*Forgets about his empty willow creel.*

*An hour has flown – or was it two or three –*
*The time for fishing past. Time to return*
*To city strife and noises, slavery,*
*The dollars for necessities to earn.*

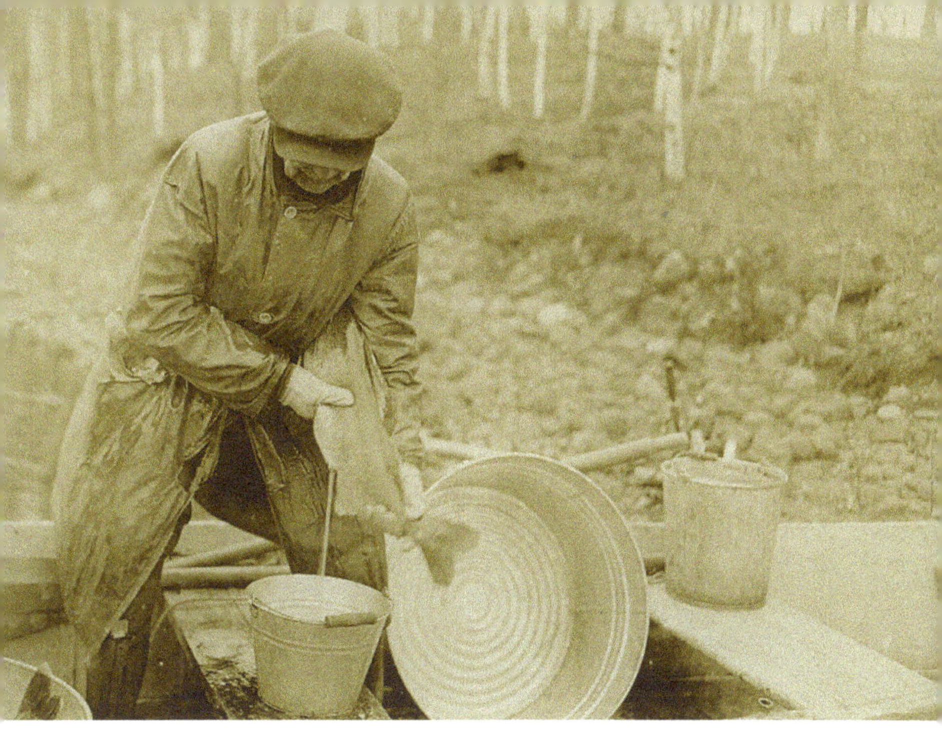

*Back home again. – "How big a catch today?*
*You took your time. They must be striking hard.*
*You'll say, I suppose, the big one got away.*
*Come over here. Let's see your catch Old Pard."*

*The creel was empty, – not a single fin –*
*And yet this radiant light in anglers eyes.*
*It showed such joyous happiness within,*
*That only nature-lovers can surmise.*

*He humbly quoted from Ike Walton this:*
*"It is not all in fishing just to fish."*

# "OLD BUCK", THE TROUT

*The trout run big in Ox-bow Bend*
*Let's go today and try our luck.*
*Let's see if we can lightly send*
*A "Royal Coachman" to "Old Buck".*
*In size he surely tops them all,*
*(Put on for years a pound a year)*
*And many are stories tall*
*Of mightly battles that one hear.*
*"Old Buck" is wise and full of tricks*
*And how to use them well he knows,*
*He winds the leader 'round some sticks*
*Then waves his tail and off he goes.*
*It seems "Old Buck" is there to stay,*
*Quite safe in deep Old Ox-bow Bend.*
*And then again – perhaps today –*
*Will "Old Buck's" reign in river end.*

*It was to be - He is no more —,*

*This grand old trout in Ox-bow Bend.*

*He fought a fight with tricks galore,*

*But today —*

*Was the day —*

*And the end.*

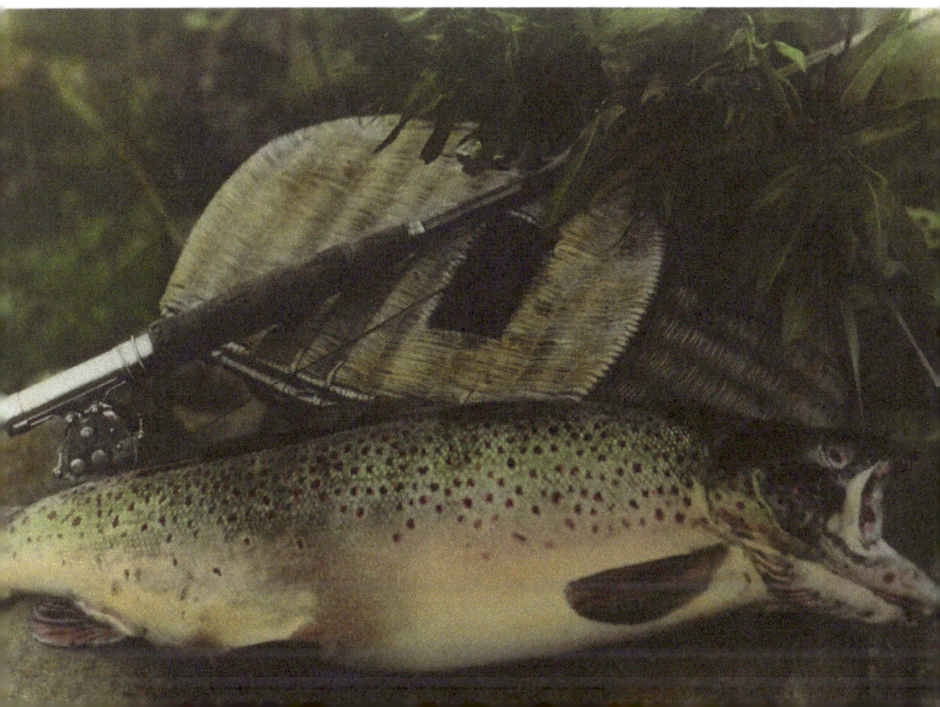

# *WOODLAND SOLITUDE*

*Woodland solitude, in velvet dressed,*
*By glow of setting sun caressed,*
*Mystic enchantment of the night,*
*Elemental beauty, tender light.*

*Woodland solitude, bloom of magic,*
*Melancholy calm and tragic,*
*Remote and baffling loneliness,*
*With infinite charm and Holiness.*

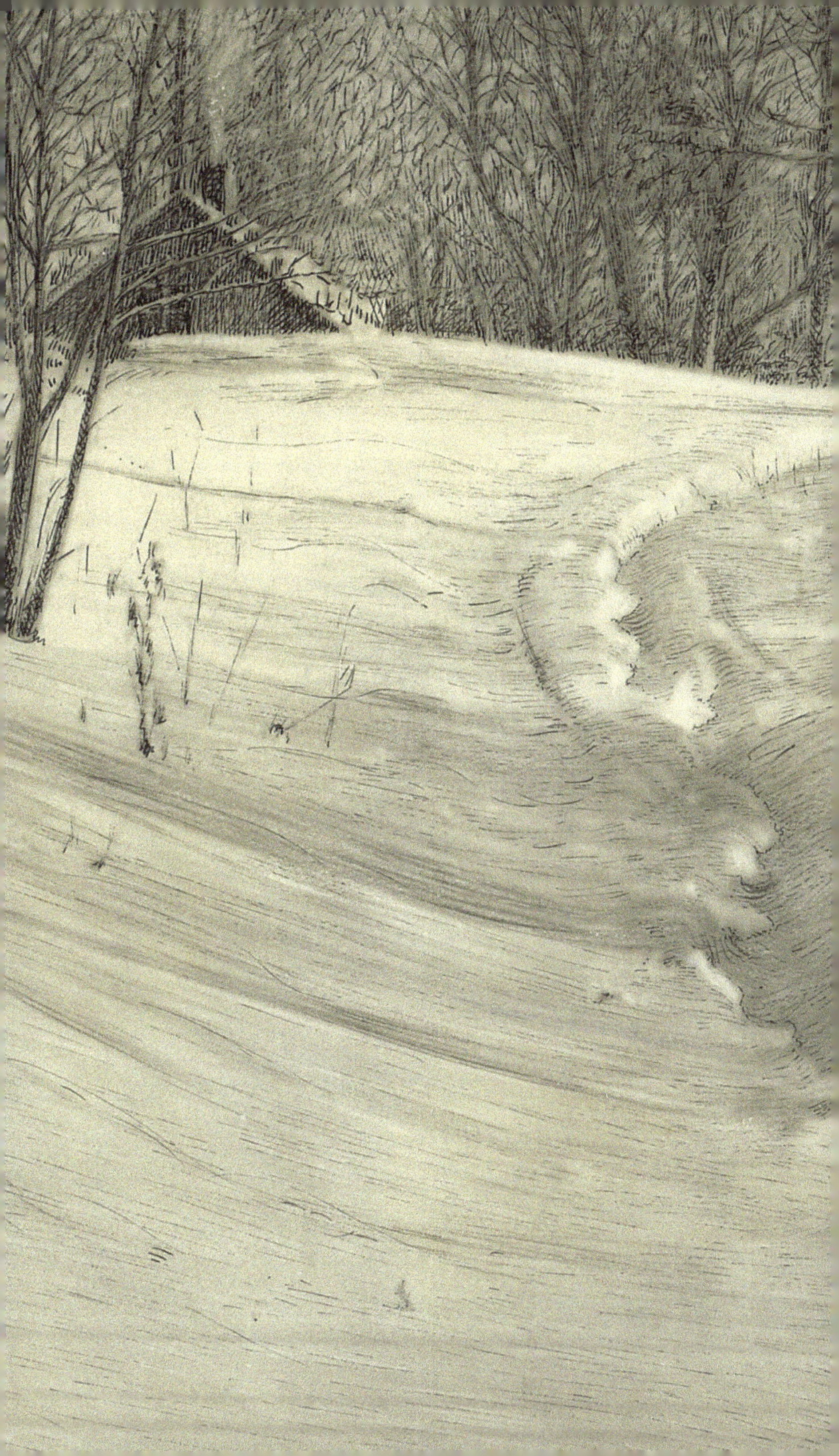

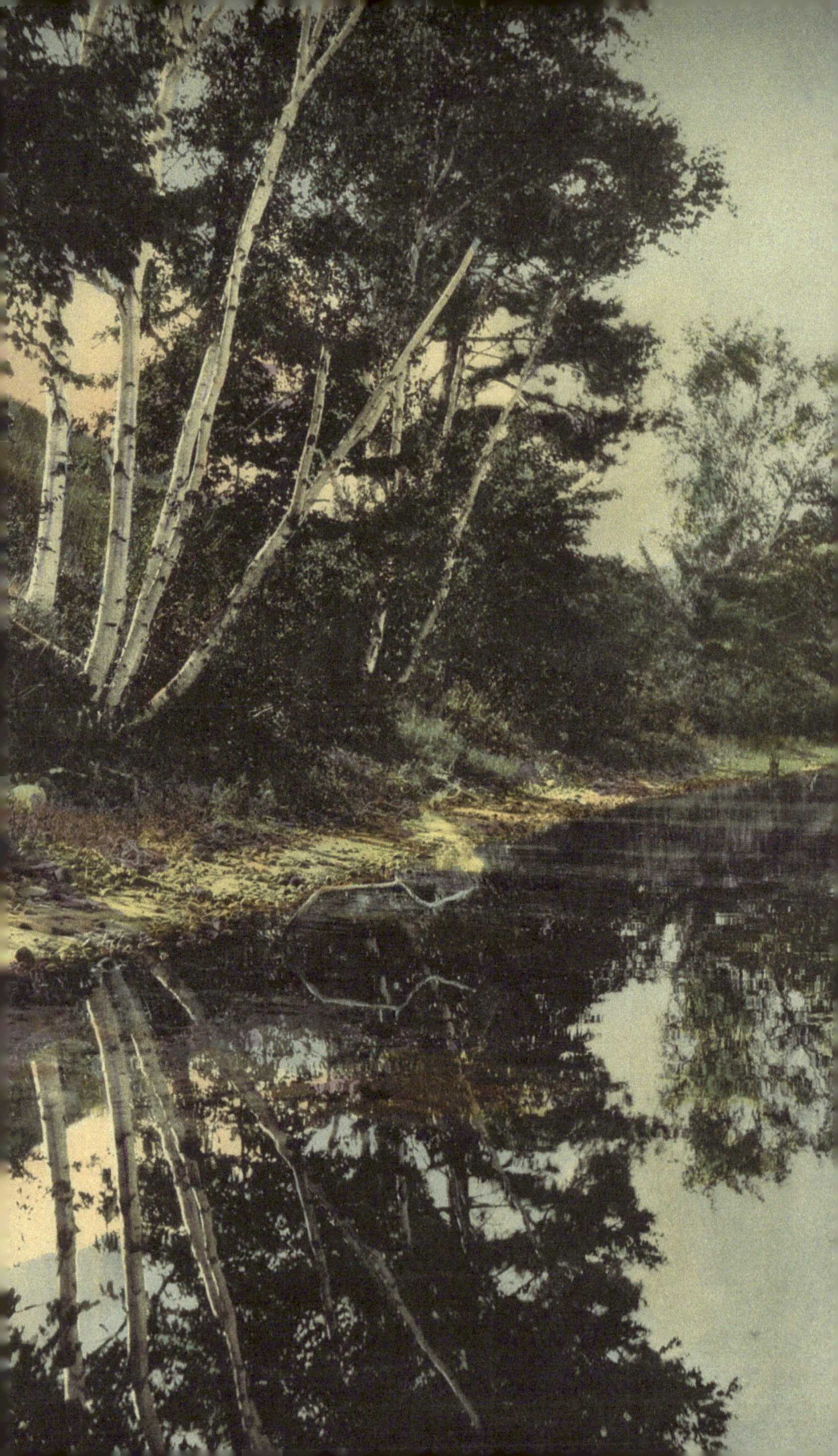

# *THE BIRCHES*

*So silvery white, in sweeping, swaying lines,*
*A graceful network limbs embrace.*
*In pale green foliage beauty twines,*
*A veil of sheerest lace.*

*So silvery white, with touch of violet, gold,*
*In sparkling newness, clean and pure.*
*An urging message they unfold,*
*Of outdoors great allure.*

# THE PINE

Here you stand on the lake shore
(For hundreds of years)
A symbolic old emblem
Of stern pioneers
And thrilling historical tales unfold
To the roar of the partridges
Thunderous drum,
While your needles so softly
A melody hum
And the whip-poor-will joins
With notes so bold.
Good Old Pine — you were saved
(From the ax-flinging hand)
And is one of the few
That remains in our land
To tell us the stories from days of old.

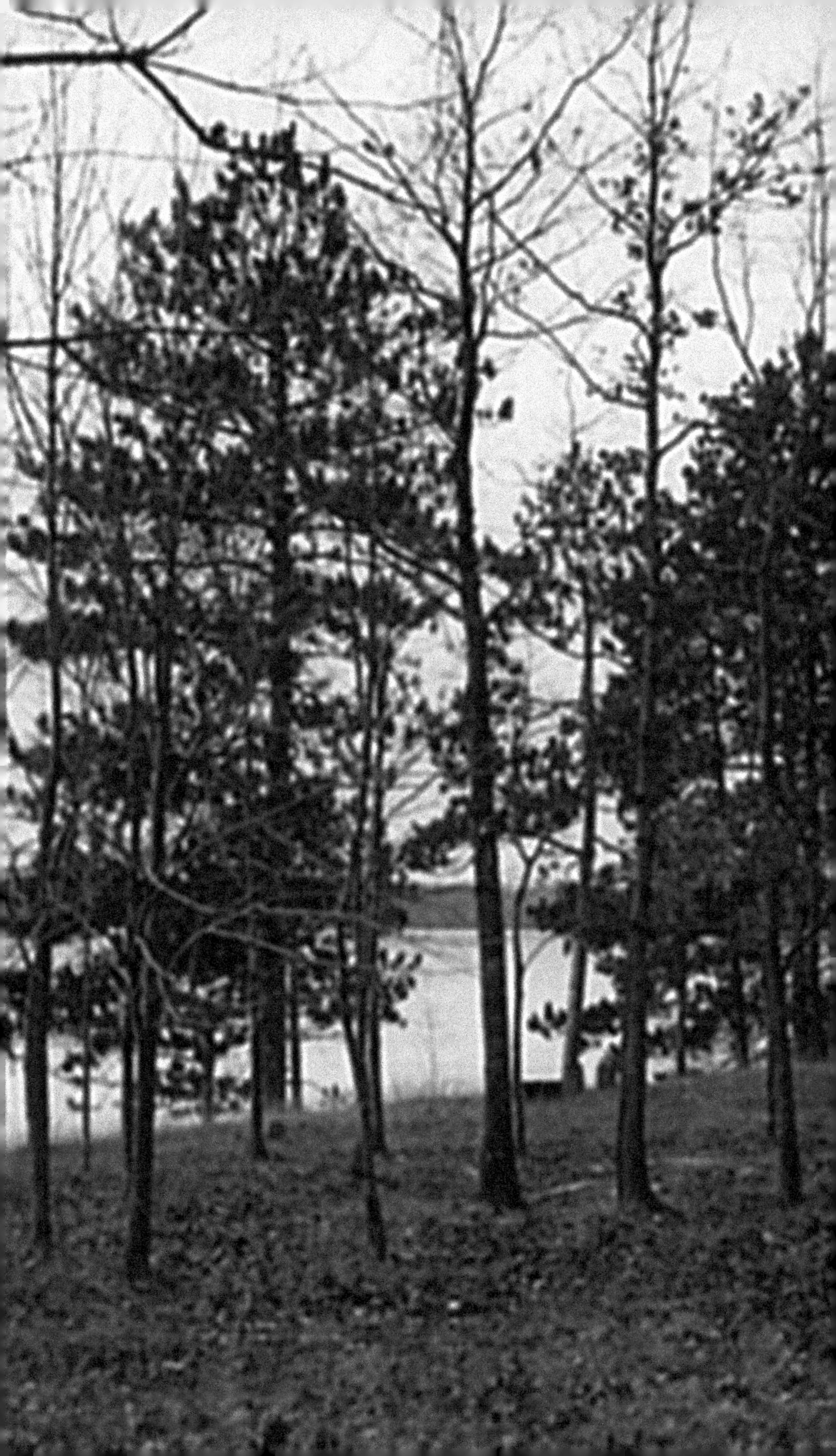

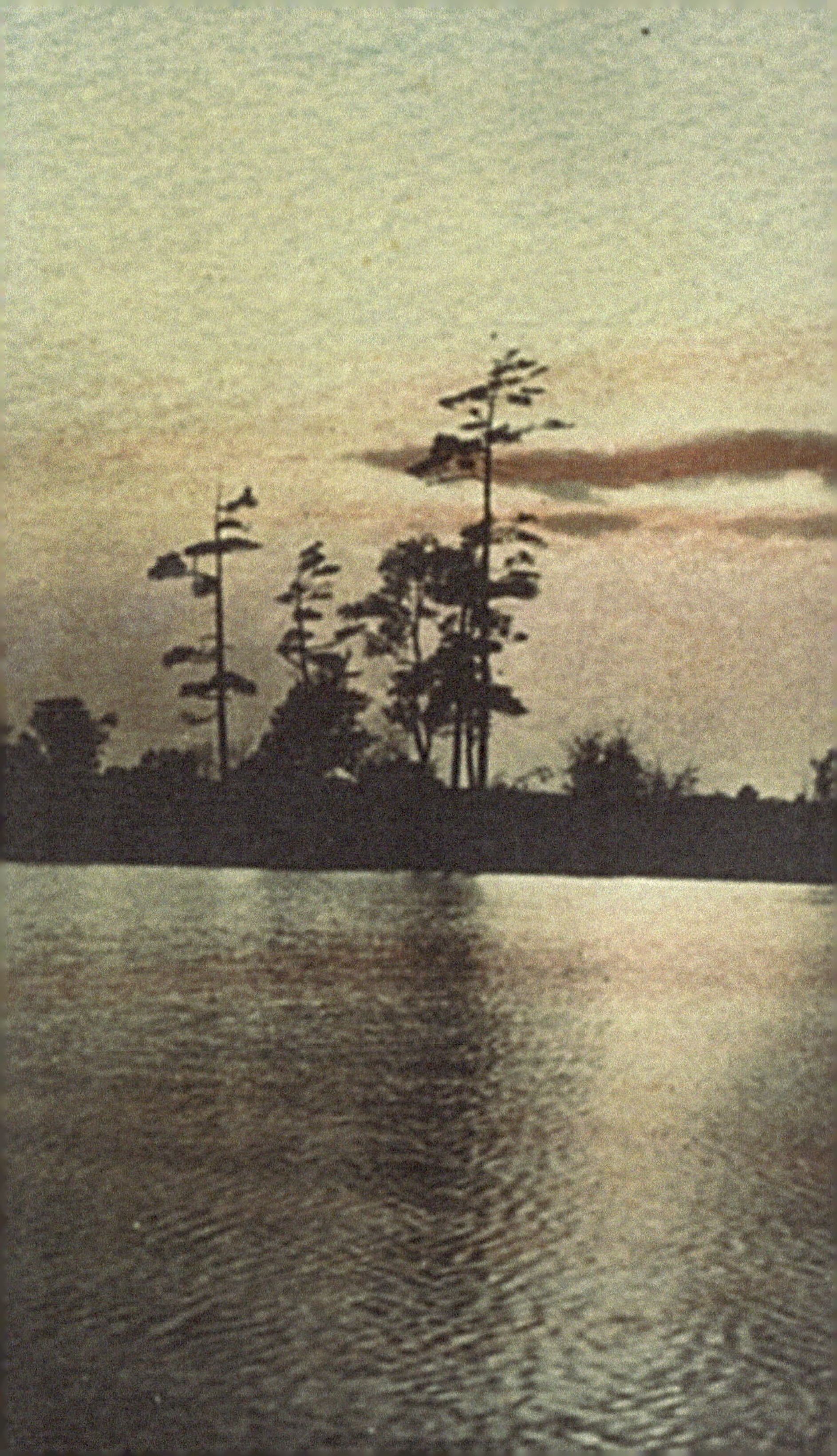

# *LADY SEPTEMBER*

*September, most beautiful time of the year,*
*When hunters start looking for signs of the deer,*
*When berries are ripe and the fishing is best*
*And Old Mother Earth in a new gown is dressed.*
*A new gown of wonderful satinline sheen,*
*Exchanged for her last one of more sober green.*
*The new tones are scarlet and crimson and rose,*
*A riot in colors indeed she chose.*
*A cheer for this girl that is topping them all,*
*This beautiful lady that comes in the fall.*

# *FROST*

*Dame Nature, through the winter months,*
*Goes on a joyous spree.*
*King Frost, the master of them all,*
*Paints every single tree,*
*With sparkling tones of white*
*And blue and rose,*
*In thousand shades*
*Of different hues that froze*
*Into a painting,*
*Glorious to behold,*
*More precious yet*
*Than all the worldly gold.*

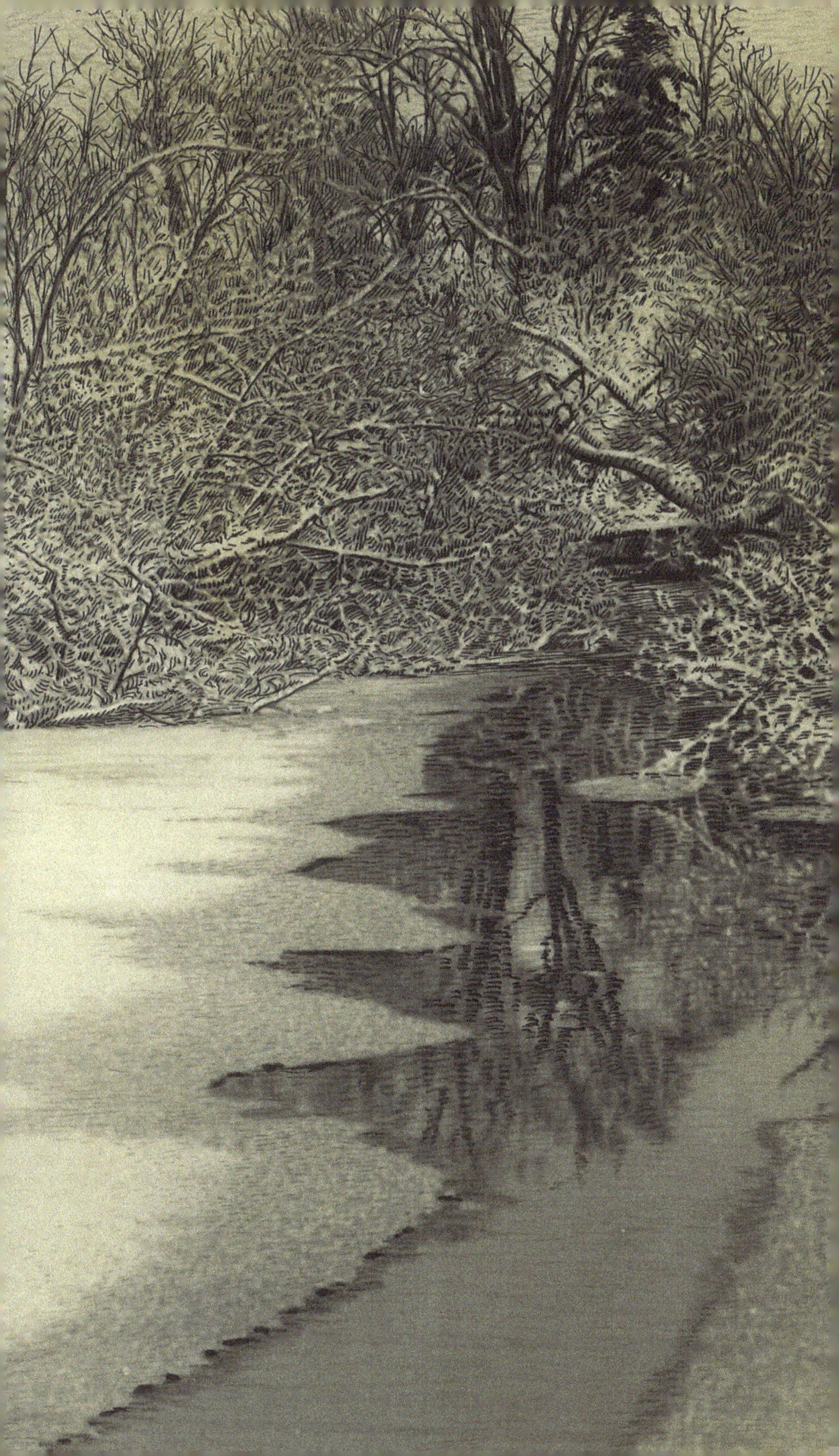

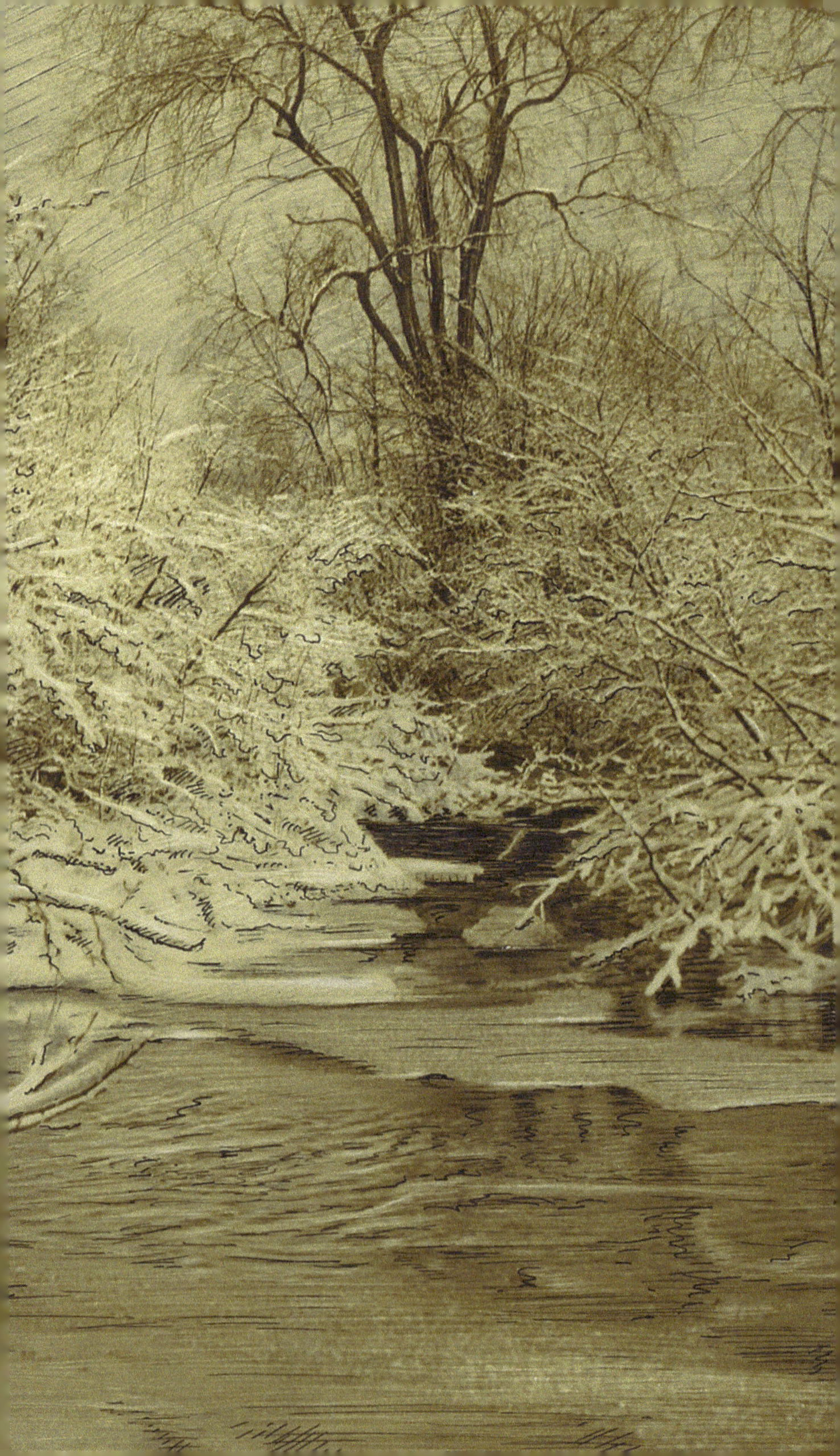

# *WINTER MORNING*

*Old Mother Earth,*
*In cloak of ermin dressed,*
*By rose-hued tint*
*From morning sun caressed,*
*Sends out this greeting*
*Over dale and hill:*
*"COME OUT THIS GLORIOUS DAY*
*AND DRINK YOUR FILL."*

# *TRACKS IN THE SNOW*

*Who made the taciturn tracks in the snow?*
*Where did he come from, where did he go?*
*Is he out for love or out for a fight?*
*This wary wanderer of the silent night.*

*Who made the mystic tracks in the snow?*
*Did he find his mate or find his foe?*
*Did he suffer death in traps set by men,*
*Or safely get back to his lair or den?*

*Baffling, mysterious tracks in the snow*
*The secrets you hold we shall never know.*

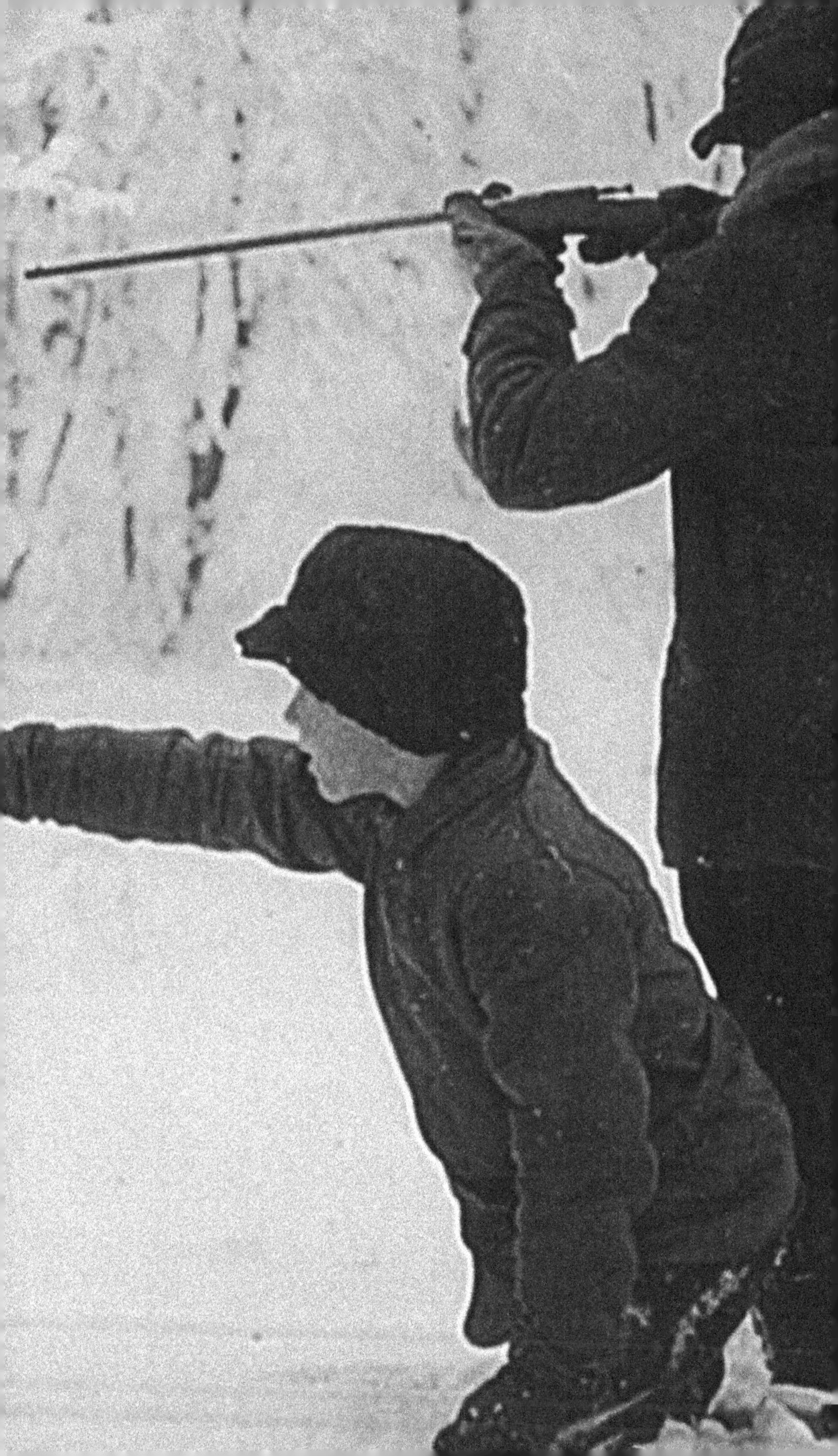

# THE WESTERN GLOW

*The western glow,*
*When brilliant day is done,*
*And clouds are tinted*
*By the sinking sun,*
*Sends rose-flushed*
*Holy Message o'er the land,*
*In beauty heralds:*
*"GOD IS CLOSE AT HAND."*

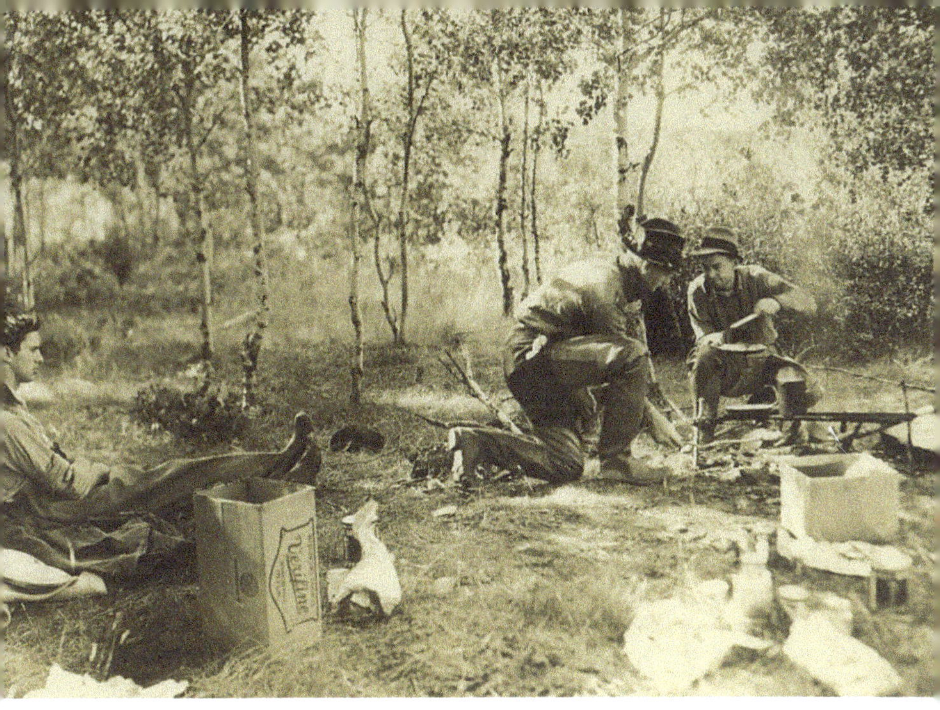

The lingering sun
Still gleams in distant west,
Day's work is done
And it is time for rest,
When Holy Solemn Radiance
O'er the land
As softly heralds:
"GOD IS CLOSE AT HAND."

# THE SUNSET HOUR

*The molten glowing sun,*
*The slow, soft wash of waves,*
*Siren against the fiery sky*
*The pineboughs sober silhouette.*
*When sunset's glorious hour is here.*

*The brilliance filters down*
*Through misty evening haze*
*And melts on slender edge of cloud*
*The priceless line of yellow gold.*
*When sunset's glorious hour is here.*

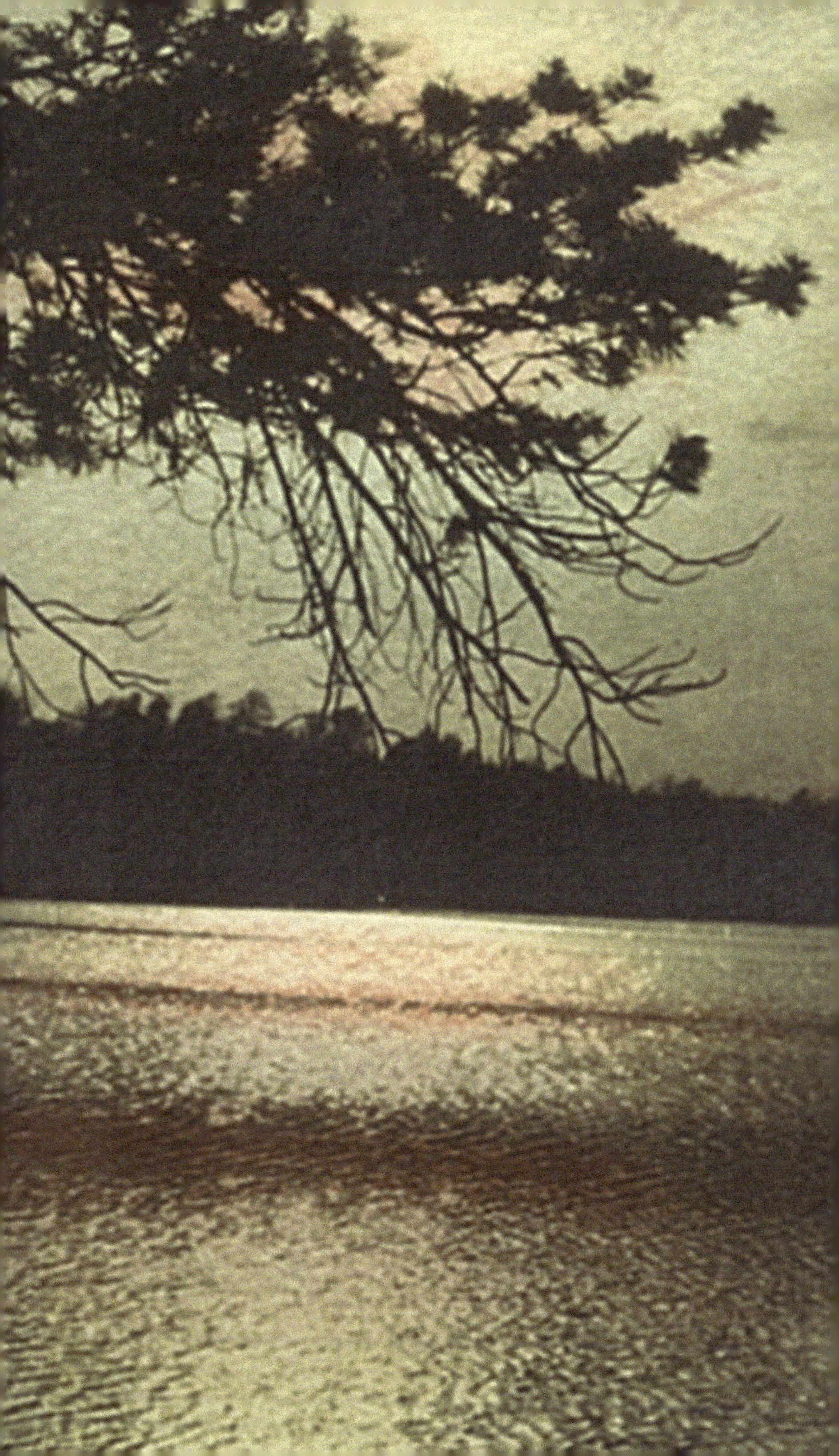

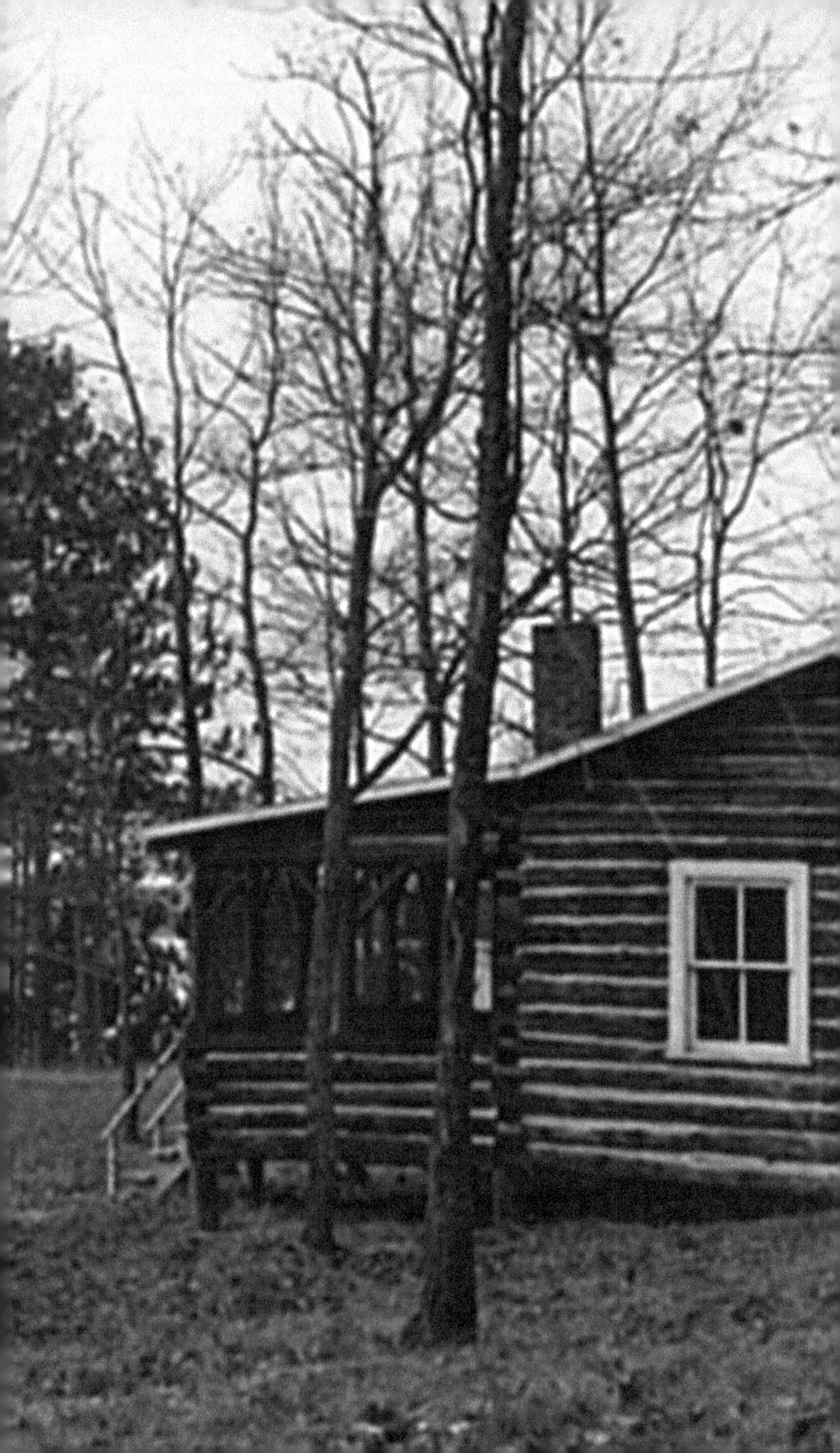

# THE EVENING HUSH

*In purple shadows, evening hush,*
*The landscape fades away,*
*In last sweet song the Hermit Thrush*
*Gives thanks for brilliant day.*

*Through misty haze of rose and blue*
*The glow of sunset gleams*
*And flickering light of golden hue*
*Is spread on luminous beams.*

*Our thoughts grow tender, fill the heart*
*With joy and hope supreme.*
*A holy peace - of God a part -*
*Our inner selfs redeem.*

# *STATION S-U-N, SIGNING OFF*

*The Sun is signing off in last refrain,*
*This splendid day will never come again,*
*It reached the final goal it set.*
*It was a day of joy and glee and cheer,*
*It was a day for tender love my dear,*
*A day we will not soon forget.*
*Another day (tomorrow) will be here,*
*Another program to enjoy my dear,*
*Perhaps more perfect yet.*

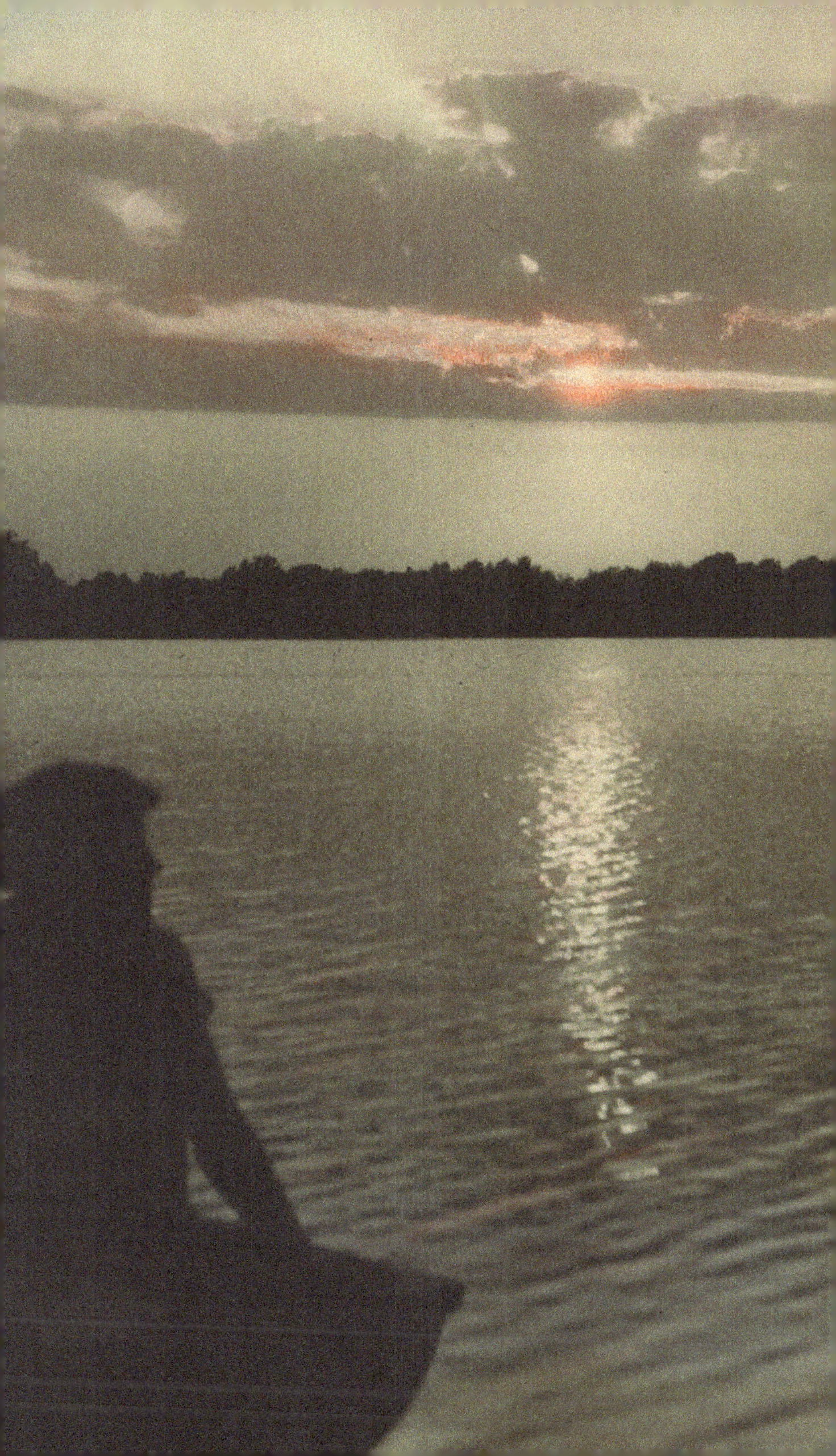

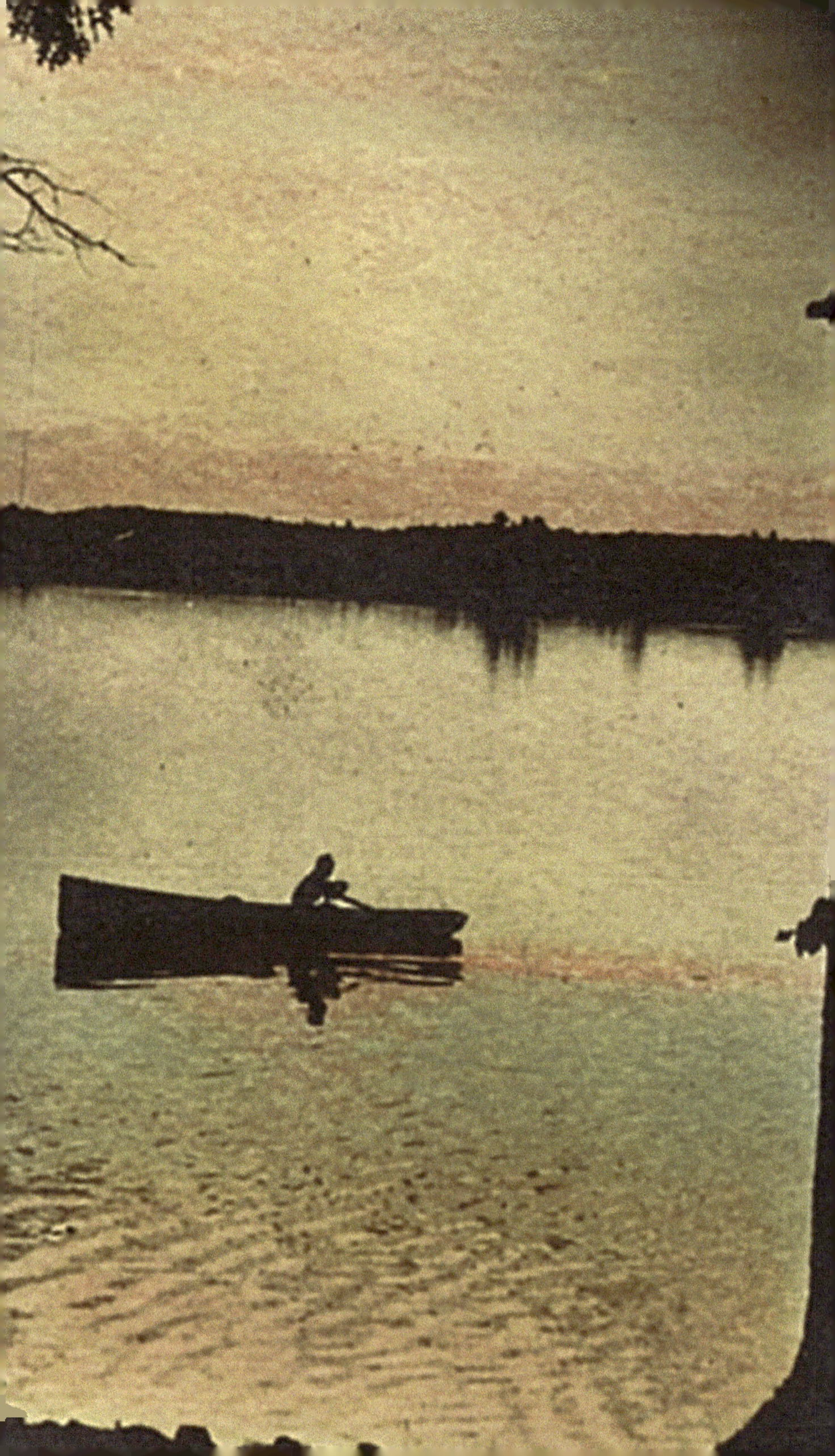

# *THE DAY IS DONE*

*A whispering breeze rolls gently 'cross the bay*
*As lingering, silent shadows creep away*
*And brilliant day is done.*
*The day turns into darkened night once more*
*And Father Time marks down another score*
*Against the fading sun.*

# NIGHT IN THE WOODS

*Enchantment of the evening*
*And the night,*
*Black velvet hands*
*Of sober pines*
*Reaching out*
*Against gleaming light*
*Of the moon.*
*The wind whines*
*A plaintive tune.*

*Wonderous night, so full*
*Of mystic thrills -*
*The wildcat's scream,*
*The treetoad's peep,*
*Whip-poor-wills.*
*The hours*
*Of stillness,*
*Noises cease.*
*Silence deep.*
*Contentment. Peace.*

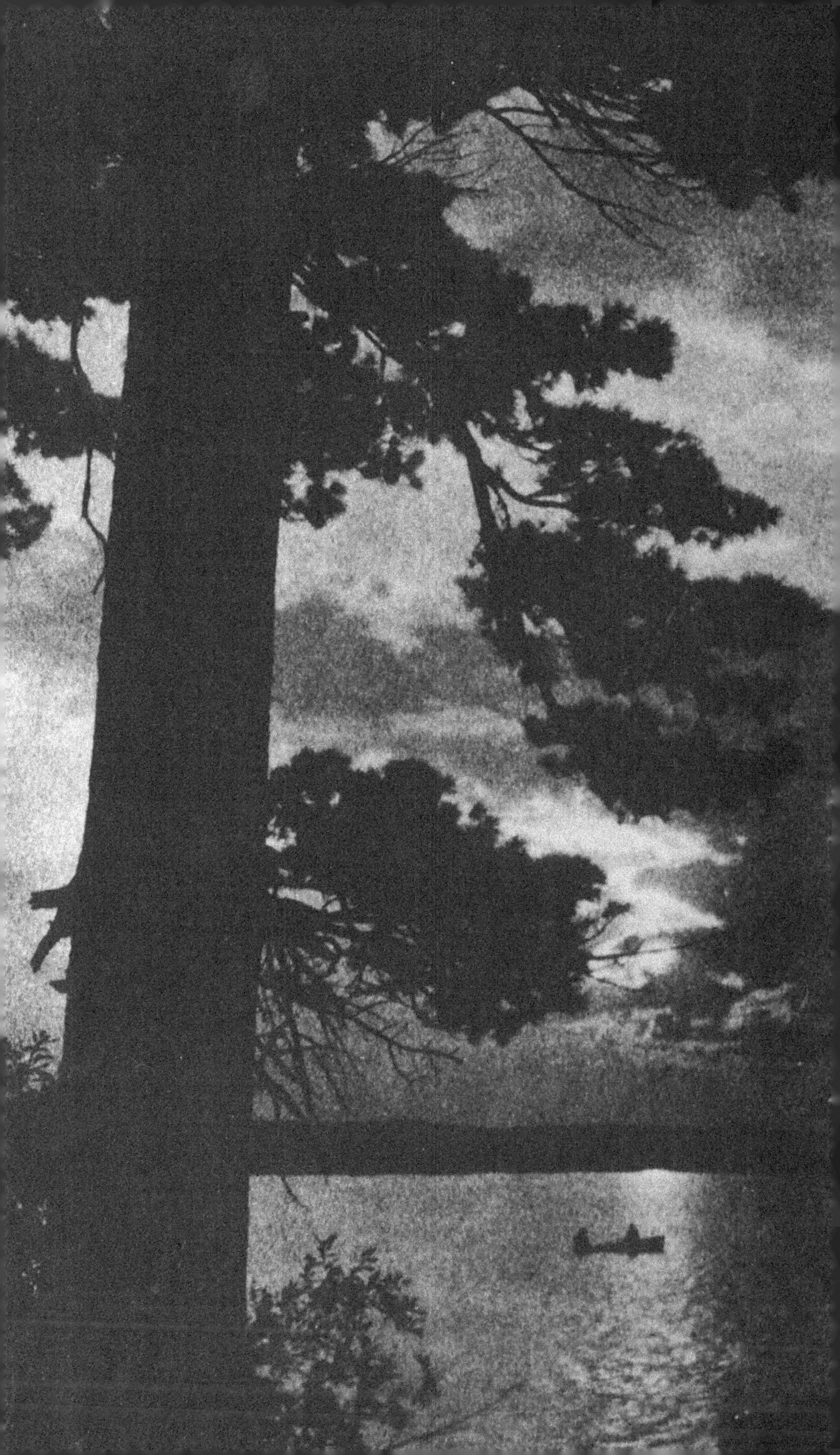

# SYMPHONY OF THE NIGHT

*At eventide, when rose-flushed clouds so gently sail*
*Across the golden path of sinking sun,*
*When brilliant light of day began to fail,*
*Then sweet appealing voices of the night begun.*

*The plover, high above, sent out his whimpering note*
*And cautiously the mockingbird tuned in,*
*So sweetly, pianissimo, remote,*
*Did sacred symphony of night begin.*

*You heard the lyric tones of frogs in lonely march,*
*Such very friendly notes with sweet appeal,*
*Then killdeer's hurried call, tho shrill and harsh,*
*Yet very charming, sympathetic, true and leal.*

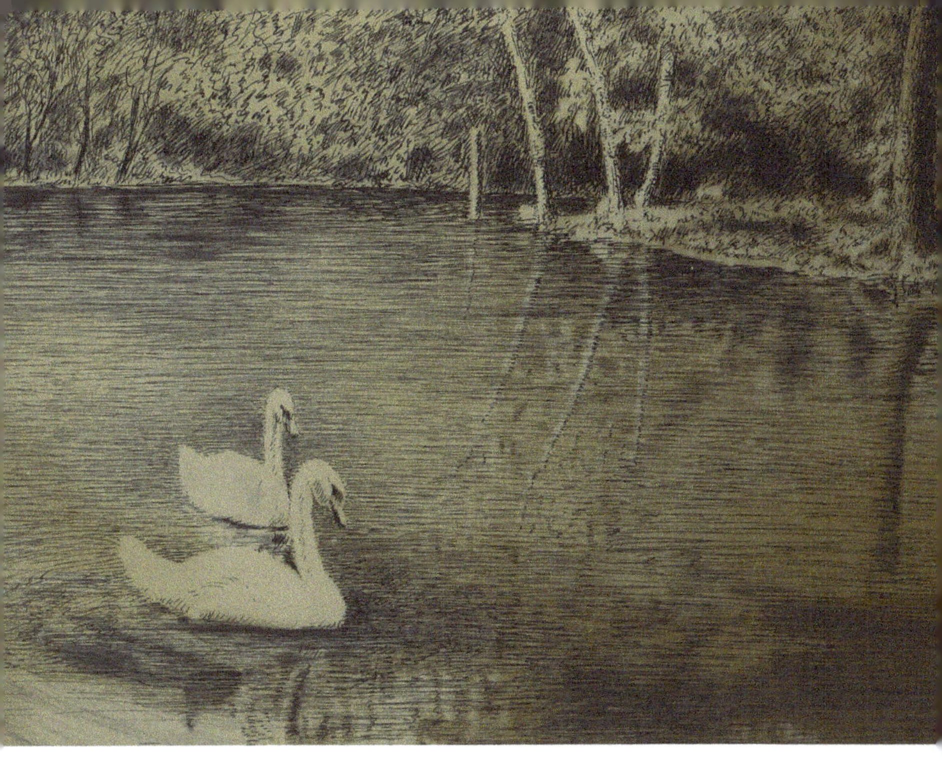

*You heard the sharp staccato scream of laughing loon,*
*— A pause — A thrilling moment of a soothing hush —*
*Then wonderous mellow sweetness of the tune*
*That flows from golden-tinted throat of hermit thrush.*

*A slight belated, fragrant breeze sweeps through the pine,*
*A whispering, lovely tune of sweet caress,*
*A classic melody through woodland shrine,*
*A symphony to heal despair of hearts distress.*

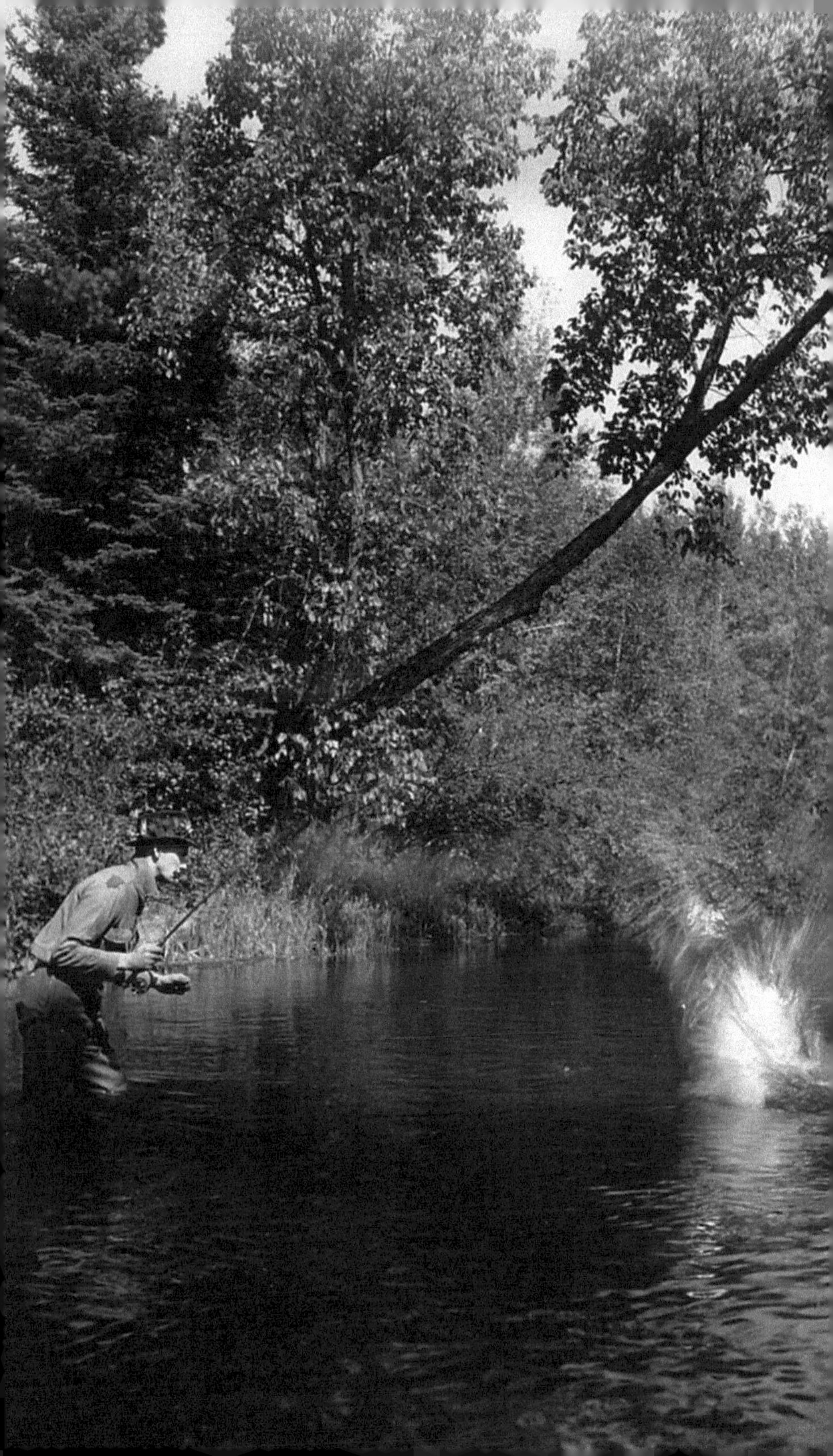

# *THE DANCE OF THE NYMPHS*

*To music played by lingering breeze,*
*In rhythm slow and waltz-time easy,*
*The Nymphs dance on with lovely grace*
*In evening gowns of misty lace.*
*All night the thrilling dance goes on.*
*While far above the moon looks on.*
*The floor of silver, ceiling of gold,*
*All splendant beauty to behold.*
*When dawn grows near on unseen wings*
*It's time to quit. When morning rings*
*And heralds yet another day*
*The nymphs as softly dance away*
*In sacred hush through fading light,*
*By dawns first rosy, glimmering light,*
*O'er Holy Path that's only trod*
*By the Nymphs, by the Aura of God.*

# *LIGHT BEYOND*

*Marvelous sky and beauty supreme -*
*Transcendent light beyond foretells,*
*Of Holy Regions that redeem*
*Our Souls from earthly shells.*

*Before you here I stand to find,*
*The problem solved. I really know*
*And feel the cry within my mind*
*That joy will overflow,*
*WHEN I REACH THE LIGHT BEYOND.*

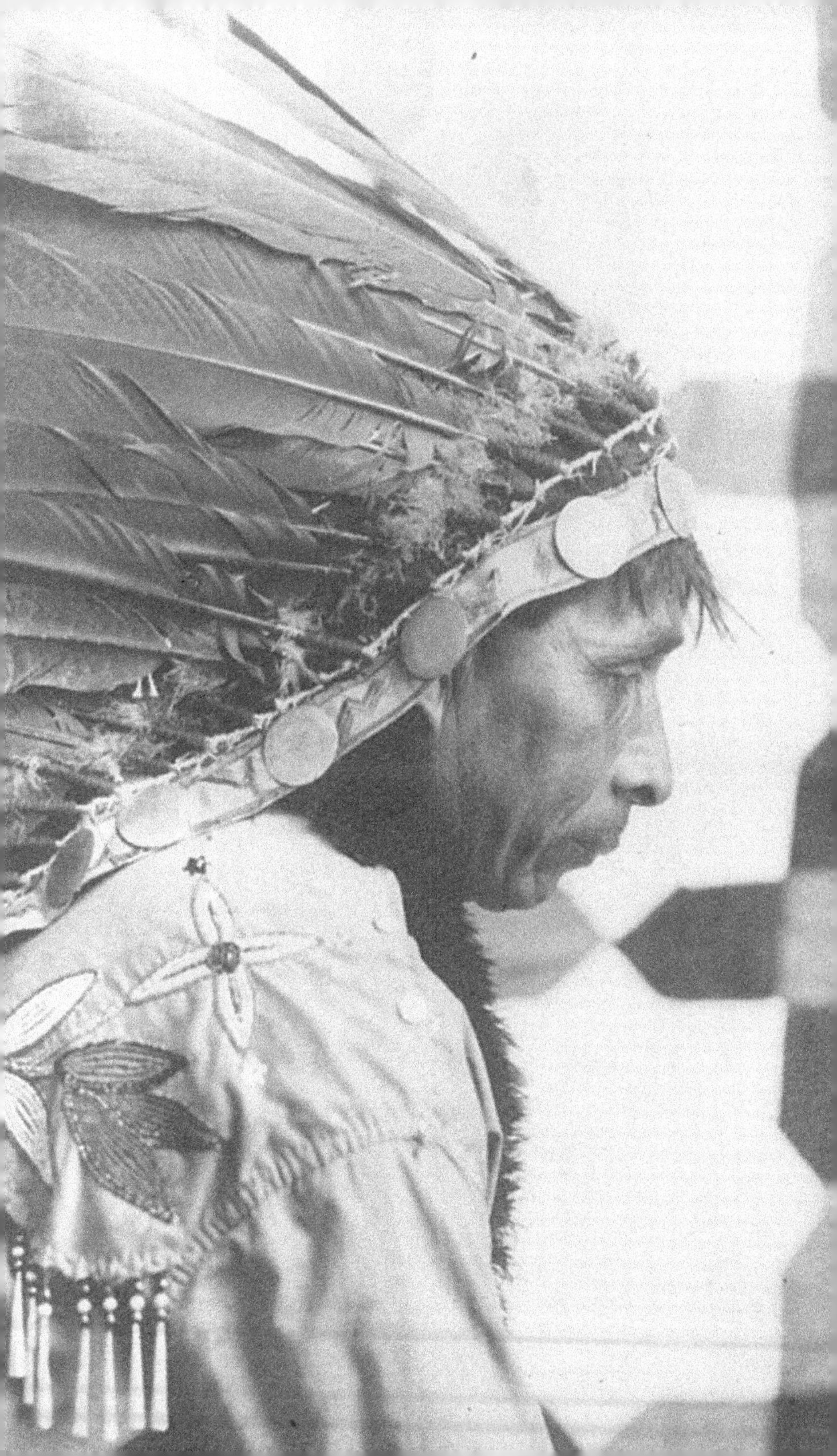

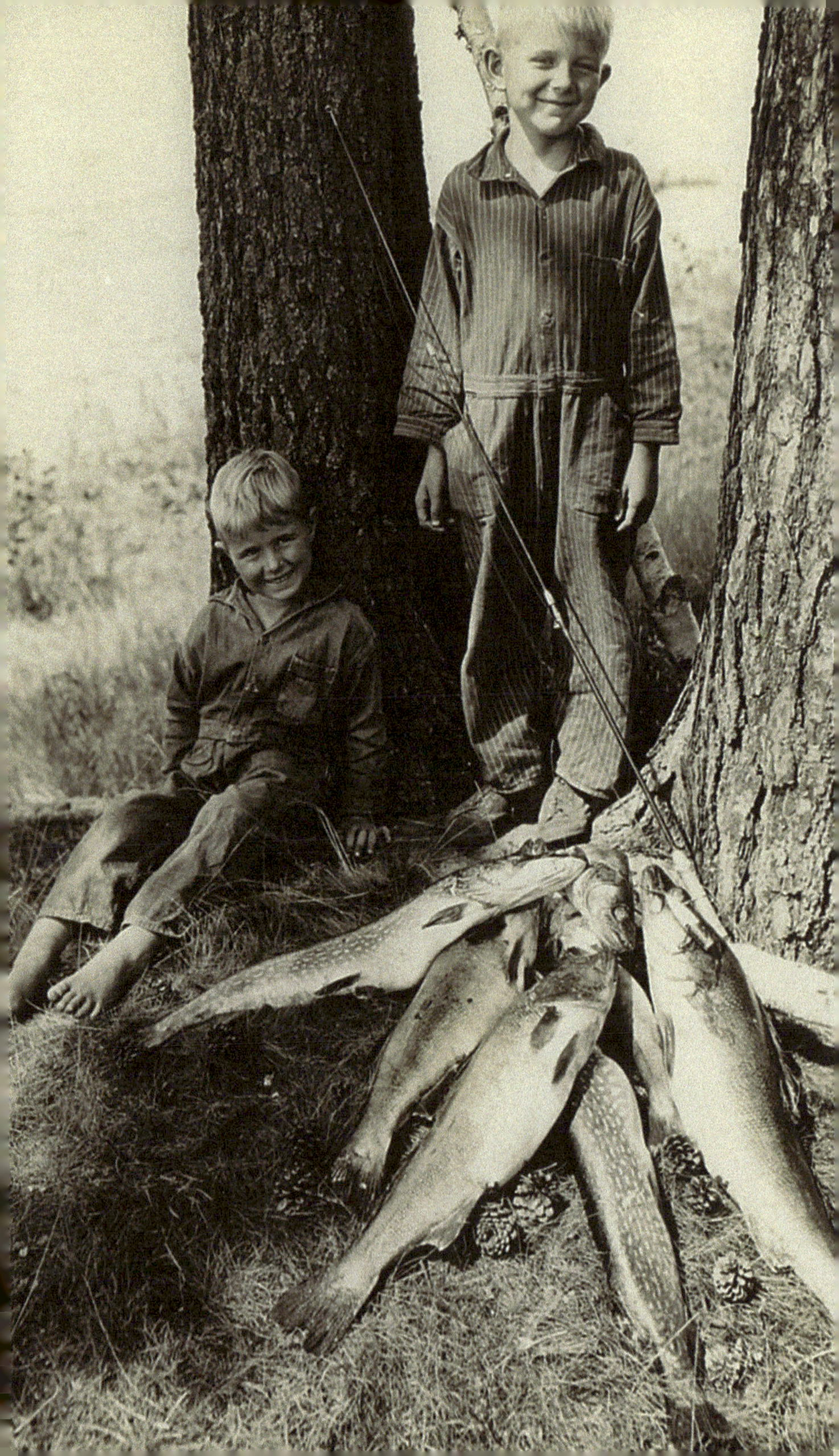

# *THE GLIMMERING PATH*

*Spread out on velvet sweep of lovely blue*
*Lies glimmering path of polished silver hue.*
*A path with countless jewels paved*
*Of precious gems, through ages saved.*
*A brilliant path in gleaming lines*
*That in the evening hush entwines*
*A sacred power that relays*
*And guides our thoughts through misty haze*
*To festive, consecrated regions farther on,*
*Far out in endless space, where lies Eternal Dawn.*
*This jeweled path conveys our hope and faith*
*That everlasting peace shall always wait*
*For every soul that comprehends*
*The message that our MASTER sends.*
*This message promises happiness,*
*For all that are readiness,*
*When comes the call from out of space*
*That time is here our LORD to face*
*And to at last enjoy the promised, glorious rest*
*And Sacred Peace by Heaven's Holy Angels blest.*

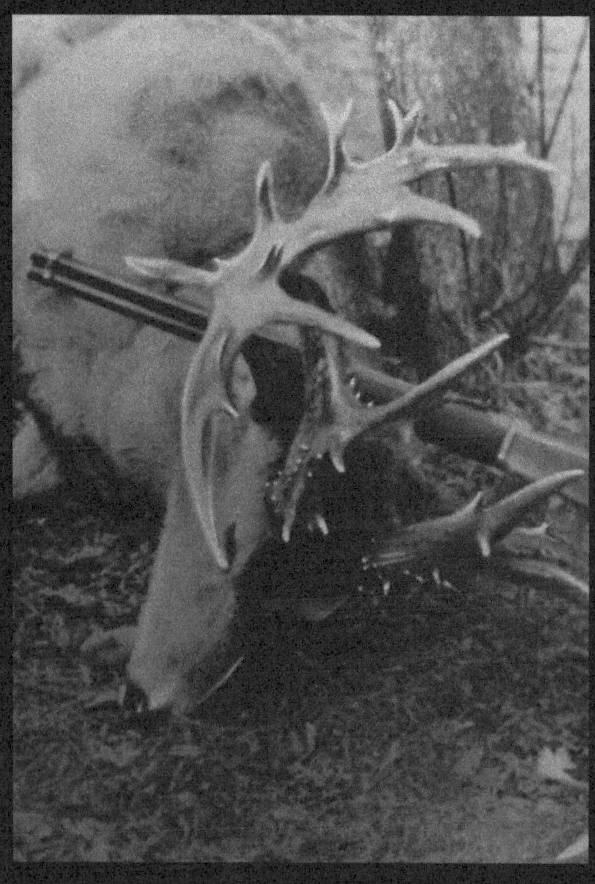

*The end is...*

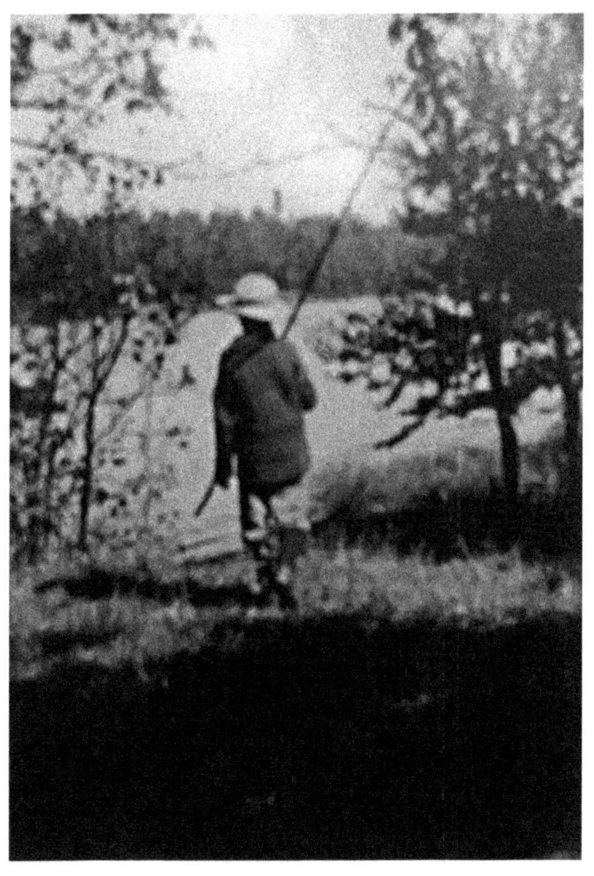

*just the beginning.*

*Sven Waldemar Swenson passed in 1938, Agnèta passed in 1970, and my grandfather Lloyd passed in 1992. Lloyd is on the cover of this book, who's legacy will continue. Thank you, Sven, and all of my family members who have passed, for allowing me to help accomplish a passionate dream, and letting this come alive with the Holy Spirit.*

*- Arlys Swenson, Great-granddaughter*

www.ingramcontent.com/pod-product-compliance
Lightning Source LLC
LaVergne TN
LVHW052357100826
845147LV00013B/861

* 9 7 8 1 6 4 5 3 8 0 3 9 9 *